BOOKWORM

ROSAMOND PURCELL

BOOKWORM

Introduction by Sven Birkerts

The Quantuck Lane Press
New York

Bookworm
Rosamond Purcell

Book design and composition by Laura Lindgren
The text of this book is composed in Simoncini Garamond.

Manufactured by Mondadori Printing, Verona

Library of Congress Cataloging-in-Publication Data
Purcell, Rosamond Wolff.
    Bookworm / Rosamond Purcell ; Introduction by Sven Birkerts.
        p.   cm.
    Includes bibliographical references.
    ISBN-13: 978-1-59372-023-0
    ISBN-10: 1-59372-023-8
1. Photocollage. 2. Purcell, Rosamond Wolff. I. Title.
TR685.P83 2006
779.092—dc22   2006020027

The Quantuck Lane Press, New York · www.quantucklanepress.com

Distributed by
W. W. Norton & Company, 500 Fifth Avenue, New York, NY 10110 · www.wwnorton.com
W. W. Norton & Company Ltd., Castle House, 75/76 Wells Street, London, WIT 3QT

1 2 3 4 5 6 7 8 9 0

To
John D. Constable—intrepid traveler and humanitarian,
Katharine Park—fearless thinker and counselor,
two wise and cherished friends.

Many thanks to Brook Wilensky-Lanford, associate publisher at
The Quantuck Lane Press; to Don Kennison, copy editor;
and to Laura Lindgren, designer of *Bookworm*.

Special gratitude to Julia Sheehan for her help with editing the photographs;
to Rikki Ducornet, Elizabeth Meryman, Lisa Melandri, Singer Editions, and
the Kathleen Ewing Gallery, for offering encouragement over the years
through the twists and turns this work has taken; to Sven Birkerts for
his generosity with words and time; and to William Buckminster
for so many objects metamorphosed into treasure.

Thanks as always to Dennis Purcell, all-time hometown hero, for his unstinting
editorial and technical support. As it was the effects produced by chewing of
much paper by tiny jaws that first brought this particular work to Jim Mairs's
attention, I salute the insects and rodents and am grateful to Jim for his
steadfast love of paper, type, and books—in whatever guise they take.

Contents

The Trained Eye

Sven Birkerts

The eye, that sublimely light-responsive capsule, would be an instrument of the purest objectivity if it were severed from the affective sensibility, but of course it never is. For that we have the camera, with its "objective" lens, but then the camera inevitably comes with its user, the affective sensibility that is its appendage. The acknowledgment of this is the beginning of the art of photography, where the lens is not assumed to be the mere neutral register of light and form but rather a way of officiating the act of seeing, the human "vision." The deeper we move into the implications of seeing, so it seems, the closer we come to thought, to vision as a recognition that things presented inevitably suggest, imply . . . mean. For some, anyway, seeing is thinking and making images of the seen is thinking raised to the level of meditation.

Taken together, Rosamond Purcell's photographs—records of the thinking eye—offer a prolonged meditation on a set of thematic obsessions. To look at a number of her works in sequence is to be drawn away into a stream of associations and recognitions that could threaten to leave the visual behind altogether were the original colors and textures of the thing itself not so brilliantly immediate.

Purcell is a witness to the profundity of ruin and decay, of the perforation of our surface world of things by time; she is a philosopher of unintended signification, of the signs and traces of the natural world that our framing attention raises up from pure meaninglessness—but to what? The photographs, of course, can't say. Purcell is fascinated, thoughtfully fascinated, by limits, boundaries, edges, the seams at which things differentiate but can also blur, run together, confuse our taxonomies. And this, too, compels her ruminating eye—classification, the mania we have for putting the singular phenomena of the world into categories, nests of likeness.

My own fascination with Purcell's vision began, as is often the case, with exposure to a single work, *Foucault's Pendulum* (page 89), a photograph introducing a series of images of ruined books, which I chanced upon at a group exhibition in Boston called "Words on Fire." I was so taken with the piece, its anomalous intensity, that I sought out more of her work, eventually inviting the photographer to be the cover and portfolio artist for *AGNI*, the literary/arts journal I edit.

My responses to that one image—to the way it invited, and then supported, meditative engagement—may be the best way for me to move in on Purcell's thematic preoccupations.

Foucault's Pendulum. At first it was just the abstract beauty that slowed and then arrested my glance. I did not yet know what I was staring at. I was drawn by way of light, color, and sharply textured shapes into what seemed to be some kind of excavation site. Right away I felt the gaping impulse, the visceral pull we all have to look into something that has been laid open to view, whether it is a building half gone to the wrecking ball or a street surface opened to its intestinal pipes. It took a moment for me to get the exhilarating double take: the mind's jarring shift from an abstract to a literal apprehension. Those marks on the bottom were, I suddenly realized, lines of print, parts of sentences, which meant, in turn, that the lit-up verticals on the left, straight as stalks of grain, were the edges of pages, that this jaggedly bit-into thing was a book. And the images mounted beside it on the wall (many of them included in this volume), many of them similarly perched on the very edge of abstraction, were likewise books.

I register double takes every day—the sidewalk mound that gathers from the certainty of a dead animal to a child's brown cap in the space of a stride; the distant lake that turns out to be the galvanized roof of a shed—and most of them don't stick. But the leaps and shifts I went through when I first looked at this artist's images are something else again. These works one after the next enacted the rarest and happiest marriage of elements. Beautiful in themselves—each an instance of the shapes and shadings of the world ambushed by the artist's eye—they also induce, in the echo-life of delayed recognition, the most provocative meditation on the defining paradoxes of the book. The vivid illumination of damage in these particular photographs—whether from rot, mold, rodent, or insect—is visually compelling; it also isolates and heightens the idea of the book as material object. We are reminded that this emblem of the mental life is subject like any other thing to the processes of erosion and decay. This is the paradox: that when a book is most conspicuously, most glaringly, a material object—in decomposition, say—it is somehow also closest to revealing its immaterial essence: its soul, the hidden weather of its signs and meanings. To pounce, as if by surprise attack, on the estranged signifier, to glimpse it out of context, is to have one's face pushed right down into the business of signification. What could be more profound? Or unlikely—that an eaten-away, a mildewed, a hammered-into print artifact should turn out to be the intimate back door opening onto the inner place of reading.

Foucault's Pendulum and other images in the series bring together the focused pleasure of aesthetic apprehension and the challenge of its deeper implications. As I later took in photographs of other objects, other parts of what proved to be a major extended oeuvre, I experienced a sequence of similar reactions. Perception chased by recognition followed more gradually by contemplation. Perception, recognition, and then, for me, the inevitable thematic aftershock awareness of the implacable nature of time, the force that undoes, breaks down, removes. The sequence is profound, and to think in terms of this force is to situate thought in the larger frame, the philosopher's sub specie aeternitatis.

I make it sound as if all of Purcell's work is about dissolution and decomposition, the breakdown of the thing. In fact there is a great deal more, but insofar as these core images establish the artist's essential transhuman vantage, I will linger for a moment, in particular, on the way that photographs such as *Obie's Phone, Book turned out of mud,* and *Dante's Inferno* (pages 101, 67, 87) make palpable, visually as well as philosophically, the intersection of the eternally opposed vectors of creation and destruction, the intersection marking a moment of stasis, poignant stasis, for within this scheme the destroying force always ultimately prevails: the burnt book crumbles away, the telephone morphs to plastic magma, the mudbook is overtaken by rot . . . Purcell has stepped in to freeze semblance before it disassembles, and her images remind us that art, as apostrophized in Shakespeare's great sonnets, is the only countering strategy we have.

Other work entertains a different paradox, offers a variant calculus. I'm thinking of decay-inflected images like *Rebus, Writing Exercise,* and *Beetle Wings* (pages 130, 124, 85), where orders are again superimposed, opposing principles clearly suggested, but where nature itself is brought—connived—to the verge of signification. I don't think that Purcell intends to make a philosophical statement or propose nature as somehow communicating beyond itself. But she is clearly—and across many fronts—possessed by the bleeding together of our arbitrary-looking arrays of signs (*Danish rebus, Bitter Store* [pages 20, 79]) and the almost sensible arrangements that can be made with details—e.g., insect legs—from the natural world.

"Arrangements" would be the pivot term here, one that leads to the other major aspect of Purcell's enterprise, which is that of the suggestive juxtaposition. Though the artist has often worked with collage, and does include a number of collage-conceived images in this book, the works I refer to stop short of the more elaborate intentionality of that mode.

What we find are quasi-surreal stagings, for example, *Owl, Trouble at the Bottom of the Old Man's Garden,* and *Luck of the Draw* (pages 91; 30, 46, and 47; 136). Suggestive objects are set at thematic angles to one another, arresting or beautiful to look at but dissonant in how they bring codes of association together.

Owl crashes what might almost be viewed as the skeleton image of flight into a constricted opening; *Luck of the Draw* uses a whimsical visual echo to initiate rueful, almost Sebaldian contemplation of the play of chance in the larger determinism of war; and *Trouble at the Bottom of the Old Man's Garden* creates a dense frontal texture of broken shells and feathers, almost concealing a bearded visage, its eyes and rounded features taking on a peculiar Archimboldesque definition.

Purcell founds her art on the strength and elasticity of the associative intelligence. If the rational mind cannot resist making its hierarchies and classifications, the affective sensibility awakens to the suggestions of resemblance. For a visual artist like Purcell likeness is a power akin to the poet's metaphor. She is endlessly interested in how the eye, the connected human eye, projects meanings and thematic resonances on specific shapes and arrangements of shape. Purcell, we come to feel, possesses each of her photographs narratively as well as aesthetically. The elements, contingent as well as arranged, are held in the tension of her deliberation.

The image *Sleeping Monkey* (page 77) is obvious, and beautiful for being so—a profile located in a seam of rock. *Rebus*, on the other hand, is deliberately arranged; it builds to concept through stages of recognition. The gaze first seizes on the staged similarity between the insect legs and the Chinese characters that mark a kind of border to the image. We experience immediate epiphanic flashes about signification, the cipher and the cipher-like, intention and inadvertency. But then, as we peer more closely, we see that the insect parts are laid upon a paper figured with leaf designs. And now the statement gets complicated, for the decorative natural image is juxtaposed with the authentic natural remnant. The former is a kind of middle ground between indecipherable signs—the characters—and meaningless, but made, proliferations of natural images and remnant insect parts arranged to mimic the characters. The photograph is highly essayistic.

I could go on freelancing along the boundaries Purcell inscribes and suggests, and this is, in a sense, her point: to compel looking into reverie. Indeed, to think about the dynamics of this transfer is to close up the circle of this necessarily brief introduction. It is to return to the idea of time. For no question, time is the conjured presence, the force, the mystery of this work. Time as the obvious agency of change, the power that pulls apart, dissolves, and corrupts, but which also yields up to the artist the beauty of vestiges, the delicacy of remnant form.

Then there is time as we grasp it in our apprehension of implied scale. To study any of Purcell's photographs is to use the medium against itself. This is no ambush of decisive moments, no arresting via "exposure" of the stream of circumstance. If most photographs look to cut into experience, Purcell's do the opposite. Patient, seemingly removed from contingency, they gather evidence of the slow mineral work of elements, the abrading that cannot be taken by any lens, that is grasped only in thought. We take in the images in deep time because they force us to. The underlying logic of presentation asks us to imagine the before and after of whatever we are looking at, to grasp deeply the continuity of natural process that has been momentarily stalled into image. Staring into any of Purcell's images we get the feeling, as in Shelley's "Ozymandias," that "the lone and level sands stretch far away." The experience is sobering, humbling, and, in its astonishing winnowed clarity, its manufacture of visual beauty, unexpectedly uplifting.

BOOKWORM

Rosamond Purcell

M y mother told me that as a baby I waved to tree boughs blowing in the wind. By this she knew that I had good eyesight. As a child I swam in sensations, which, when I began to collect them, included such phenomena as a wrought-iron bulldog, a polished floor, dark pines, the sound of waves coming in the window, and, from a big shell, the blank hum of an alternate sea. When I was three, I had imaginary companions. Someone, either I or they, could speak in muffled tones, faint as images of ferns rising up on photo-sensitive paper set in the sun.

Long before I learned to read, I wrote a letter by making scrawled marks on paper. It looked so much like writing that I asked my mother to read it.

The first verbs we read in *Dick and Jane* are my kind of verbs:

See Spot run!

Look, Jane, see funny funny Dick!

But Dick and Jane were not my kind of friends. I stared at the pictures of Jane in her pink and blue and Dick in businessman brown. With relentless good cheer they gave nothing in return.

Some of us were overstimulated by the very concept of pronouns. "When you speak to me," ordered a friend in the first grade as we hung around after school, "you must say 'she said.'" And when she spoke, she added, she would end with "I said." I would then be permitted to speak again. I pointed out that she was not the only "I." Nor was I "she" to me. She insisted that as I was "she," I must say so, and just then (for example) I had not.

In the early grades we saw newsreels, which always began with the RKO radio tower perched at the North Pole flashing lightning bolts in all directions. The jumpy footage, often taken from the vantage point of an open trap door in a plane, featured bombs dropping on cities such as Dresden or Cologne during the last days of World War Two. We witnessed explosions, crashing planes, and always fire in these films. But as that war was now history, we were learning about the past from the news of the day. We crawled under our desks for air-raid drills not because the Nazis were coming but because the Russians might.

Throughout my school years, I loved seafaring stories. The family library included a number of books about children incarcerated in boarding school or orphaned (or at least motherless), with unsatisfactory guardians. Some, like Alice, journeyed to alternative worlds, passing over symbolic thresholds, traveling on the back of the north wind, or, like the protagonist of *The Cuckoo Clock*, through the bird's velvet-lined box. No matter how grueling the plots, these books were staunchly Victorian domestic fare, for even pirates have their own— if vicious—routines.

I read on two levels—for the words and again for the pictures. I preferred swinging along, negotiating the wide-open spaces of plot without illustrations, inventing these in a kind of simultaneous translation technique—reading and seeing—a two-ply trick. Distracted by whatever illustrations did appear, I would also read the book through for the pictures alone, and so formed two story lines. The scenes I had invented were now trumped by the artist. I was riveted by how the characters *looked*: what they were wearing, how tall, how beautiful, what their tears, their shoes, looked like. I stared into the shadows, into the distance, at the sea or the trees. In the theater, too, tracking the diurnal and nocturnal passage of time, I gave and still give my heart to the set—falling leaves, dawn and

dusk, a dungeon wall, shadows passing a translucent pane. Here, as a spectator I am truly "chewing the scenery."

Sometimes, as a special treat, our father would pull out an old travel book of Ethiopia to show us engravings of the African flora and fauna including a huge banana tree, a snarling hippo (called "the river horse"), and a spectacular spread of three Franciscan monks on a beach being beheaded by the soldiers of a Turkish emir. Scarier still was the fold-out plate entitled "Sexcenti Equites Noctu Fugitivi et viarum ignati de rupe praecipitantur." Six hundred horsemen fleeing by night . . . ignorant of the precipice that lies ahead. You could tell it was night because of the thickened engraved lines in the sky.

The riders in the rear, with lances raised, race as a wave toward the edge of the cliff, destined to be transformed, seconds later, as the wave crashes, into separate beings and singular events: a flailing horse, a boy in mid-fall, a warrior spread-eagled above the rocks sixty feet below. I could see what was *going to happen*—future, present, past of the riders—driving forward, midair, limbs reaching for the sky. There was a mountain in the background and, beyond, a mesa. There had to be houses there and people sleeping who did not know what was happening here. I entered into the farthest corner of the engraving to invent what might happen next.

Years later I asked my father to find the picture of the *monkeys* falling off the cliff but we couldn't find them. Instead, again in the big book, we found the horrific scene of the racing army. Where then did the monkeys come from? In *Doctor Dolittle*, the first in a series about a doctor who speaks the languages of the animals, written by Hugh Lofting, an obliging band of long-limbed monkeys forms

"John Dolittle was the last to cross"

a bridge over a gorge to help the doctor (along with his personal entourage of animals) flee a village of angry African natives. No one falls. No one dies. This is a social parody, not a record of historical disaster. Coincidental details between the Ethiopian drawing and the rescue staged by the monkeys—escarpment, Africa, figures fleeing or racing toward a goal—produced a visual convergence and an overlapping in my memory of these pictures.

Decades later, in the natural history museum, I photographed primate skins including the hide of a gorilla from the Cameroon that I hung backlit in a window. It took considerable effort to hoist the gorilla onto the hook. Creased in the middle, like a large blanket preserved in arsenic, the hide weighed perhaps twenty pounds, immense and malodorous. I remember the smell more than I do the photography. At first he (and I thought of the ape as a male) stood alone, but

as I constructed more intricate scenarios the ape passed through various incarnations as a principal actor. It reminded me of the double portrait that featured two boys, one a ghost and the other with a scratched-out, blackened face, and I saw that its shape was an everyman kind of shape. When I began to use pictures of bombed-out buildings from World War One, the gorilla was ready to go on the road, to work as a journeyman, as favorite phrases might be used and repeated by a writer. The silhouette of the ape appeared in churches, arcades, and trees. He was there again as an enigmatic suicide in an ongoing melodrama (page 128). As both victim(s) and murderer(s), he swung as a sacrificial hanged figure that was repeated, too, in the shapes of men on horseback galloping away (pages 128, 129). As these scenes evolved so did the ape's status. At times he loomed, portentous giant, in every drama. Yet by appearing over and over in different places, he was, in time, like a coin much rubbed, reduced from a giant to a gesture. Other figures—cattle and birds—turned from beasts into marks, subsumed in the end into a larger context where, exhausted, they vanished.

In my twenties, sitting on the back porch I am trying to write a short story for college. I am *writing* this picture—writing the pool of water and the glass-topped table that contained the water and also threw it down as a shadow shot through with concentric rings of light, shaking as the breeze came, and oozing, morphing into amoebas, coronas, and deep pooling dazzle as I stepped into the scene and poured more water on the glass. Back in class the professor said, "This has no voice."

Later a friend, reading, said, "This is a picture. You know, you should be a photographer." So I took pictures, and at first they did not look anything like what I was thinking. The camera and I do not have a symbiotic relationship. I may care all I want to about what I see, but the camera is a machine and does not know how I feel.

Recently there has been a revived interest in nineteenth-century spirit photography, those images that seem to have captured beings from the beyond. Self-appointed mediums of spirit photography practiced many tricks. When I train the camera on a stone, the bark of a tree, a roll of burned tinfoil, I think I know what will appear on film, but sometimes shapes emerge I had not anticipated.

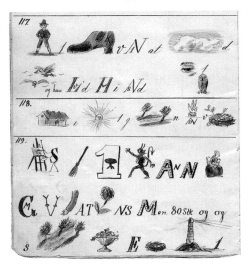

Focused attention is not enough to prevent the imagined, the invisible from showing up in the end: an angel, a crow, a Greek island. When these improbable intruders appear I act as if I knew they were there all along. "The incorruptible Kodak," wrote Mark Twain, "is the only witness that I have been unable to bribe."

The shifting roles a shape can play are like shadows on a sunlit wall; they are like sounds sliding into words and completing phrases. In a rebus, letters, syllables, and pictures come together as a single language forming a coherent whole. A rebus often forms an aphorism or saying, as in, "The devil makes use of idle hands."

Here, from *Owls Head*, about a place I came to haunt and to collect ruined objects from, is a description of the kinds of books I found:

> They run the gamut from gently weather-beaten to hard-core metamorphosed, from faded volumes that can more or less be deciphered to books that resemble shells and rocks and beyond, to rocks that look like books . . . a poetry book unfurled to the rain . . . has a clotted look, like wet wool, as words, letters, and syllables swell. Some words are now elongated, some lines swung round ninety degrees. Verses slide away under the rain dragged by the weight of paper into gullies and pulp dikes. The book slumps to the touch, malleable as clay, its lines broken in half into crooked *J*s and *L*s, mushed *M*s, *T*s, and independent commas. Liberated letters gather like the limbs of insects at the base of the churned-up embankments, and as the book dries, real insects—silverfish, sow bugs . . . tiny ants will join them. The poems metamorphose into concrete poems, the original strophes transformed into the cryptic warp and drift of paper and ink.

Many of these books, now dry and cracking, are in my studio today. Sometime in the late 1950s, one of my (exasperated) teachers observed of my style as a student that "her fondness for collecting extraordinary items sometimes causes her to be carried away by the irrelevant." By "extraordinary items" she must have meant "notions" or "ideas," for I was not, as far as I know, collecting any single *thing* back then. Whatever objects I do collect now, I do so because of the ideas they generate (pages 99–109).

Do not misunderstand; I love books. I love them whole and unprovoked. I cherish them in perfect condition and care, too, for the not quite pristine. I do not open books very wide; the cracking of a spine is an awful sound, and I turn a book with pages splayed down—as someone said, "only with mysteries." I have written elsewhere that holding a venerable book, like a beloved pet, is to feel the heartbeat slow. I pillage only those books already in an outlaw condition, those visited by termites, silverfish, mice, moths and beetles, damp, mold, rot, or fire. The tenacity of pages and bindings to survive such assaults seems miraculous.

In the natural history museum there are drawers of fossils wrapped in papers that have nothing to do with their contents. Once, layered between delicate fish slabs, I found deposit slips from an Austrian bank. A few words had transferred from the slip to the specimen. The slab from the Solnhofen limestone now read, along with its designated museum catalogue number, "Gold" and "Oesterreich." That, just by chance, words can jump ship, transferring vocabulary from one world (commerce) to another (paleontology), creates the feeling that boundaries between any two disciplines may be crossed.

Following endless seasons photographing in natural history museums and inspired by numerous fantastic juxtapositions of things and texts, I began to fabricate my own combinations of words and fragmentary bits of *naturalia*— insects, birds, fishes. Although certain assemblages look like the cover or pages of a book, these texts are made from fragments just as illegible as the letter I wrote before I'd learned to read.

The games I get to play include the constant renaming of things based on appearance. In *Cocoons* (page 123), I imagined that petrified shells could metamorphose and hatch. Here the fossil bivalves cradled in termite-eaten text exhibit the same hairline cracks as the lace-frail paper that envelopes them. The weight of each shell is considerable; the paper dissolving between my fingers, nothing. If a crack in enamel looks like a rip in paper, it is that rip. Paper tears, eggs hatch.

Reports of interspecial breeding date from ancient times. Helen of Troy— daughter of Zeus disguised as a swan and Leda, a human—was hatched from an egg, as were her siblings, Castor and Pollux and wicked Clytemnestra. Before recent centuries (and, in some places, even now) there was much confusion about the origins, relationships, and mutability of living things: a woman risked giving birth to a very hairy child if she dared gaze at a picture of a bear before that child's birth; live geese would hatch from barnacles, insects rise spontaneously from dust or water or fire, and small mammals (such as Norwegian lemmings) rise from the damp earth or fall from a cloud.

Such mutable origins come from a nonscientific world of metaphor, of sympathetic rather than biological affinities. This was a world in which, as the author Mary Campbell writes in *The Witness and the Other World*, every natural event had a figured equivalent about which even learned men would be sympathetic to "God . . . as an author, history as a fable, the hooting of an owl as augury."

Spontaneous generation is a jolly event, a fecund force: mayflies rising from the water, dragonflies from fire, tadpoles from the mud, rains of frogs and fishes from the sky. The crystallized egg yolk (page 141) glows with the fire of life. When it regenerates, however, it will emerge not as a chicken but as a mass of maggots, which, to the naked eye, seem to have magically appeared.

Convergence is a phenomenon that offers infinite entertainment to anyone amused by coincidence of forms. In one collage (page 136), the spade on the playing card is repeated by the bombs; the French village (page 139) with its piece of rust like fire rising is echoed by the swollen orchid in the book (page 138)—as the moths look like musical notes, the legs of beetles look like letters, and elsewhere all primates look like men. Because the materials are by no means perfect, the boundaries between them are cracked and pliable. Without compunction, I bring them together, making assumptions about what looks like what; I see faces where there are none (page 77), make connections between letters and the limbs of insects, and group together objects that share a most general descriptive feature like "Holes."

The collection of things with holes includes the opening in a picture frame, nails driven into a book, stony projectiles made of cooling lava, abrasions left by

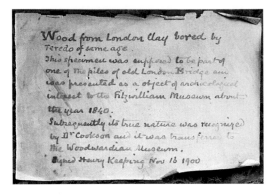

the effects of the poison PDB used to kill insect pests, holes in a piece of antique bread, air holes in metamorphic rock showing the profile of a monkey, the damage to the wood of London Bridge by shipworms, and the unwrapped packet of buckle tongues from an eighteenth-century brass foundry. The wood and the bread are authentic historical artifacts, their labels included here for further edification (page 75). Another object of unusual provenance, though unlabeled, is a silk powder puff on a stick (page 150) found wedged in a broken windowpane. It had belonged to Christina Olsen, subject of *Christina's World* by Andrew Wyeth.

The moths with wing spots that match musical notation (page 96) are reminiscent of the moths that over the decades evolved dark sooty wings to match the dirty telephone poles they clung to in northern England.

In 1989 I enlisted the help of Dr. James Traniello, biologist and proprietor of a university-sponsored termite colony, to guide the insects in the foraging of carefully selected pages of text that I then used as elements in the assemblages (pages 92, 93). The termites preferred to eat when the papers were layered with moistened birchwood (page 84). They ate the pages by tracing contours of moistened paper, and their foraging patterns left decorative cartographic islands, hollows of text not unlike Pacific atolls shaped by coral growth or the layering of sedimentary rock in western American landscapes. These patterns are mesmerizing, exhibiting as they do a fractal beauty (page 89). I offered up to Traniello's colony selected architectural texts, pages of perspectival drawing, a Dutch version of the Book of Genesis, and a catalogue on handguns. It took several weeks for these termites to consume even a small stack of pages. We discovered that they did not care for certain inks, rejecting, for example, a picture of a tomato dyed a luscious orange in an otherwise black and white gardening pamphlet, though they did consume the descriptive text in its entirety. And once, when Traniello had been out of town at the end of a critical cycle, I received bad news about fresh-gnawed papers I was poised to retrieve. "Sorry," he said, "they ate the whole thing."

Professor Michelle Pellissier Scott, a biologist whose research covers all aspects of the *Nicrophorus*, the burying beetle of northern New England, has long encouraged my construction of pseudo-collections. In 1989 Dr. Scott cheerfully supplied me with the bones of mice and small birds, the carapaces and limbs of beetles, all collected in the line of duty. It wasn't until sixteen years later that I was witness to the biological strategy practiced by two adult *Nicrophorus*. In the summer of 2005, in northern New Hampshire, my husband and I watched as a pair of burying beetles (no more than three-quarters of an inch long) turned a dead mouse (more than three inches long) over and over down the porch steps, interring it under soil and leaves. Underground the beetles would raise their young inside this mouse, feeding them as they grew.

A bookworm is a burrower. The insect boxes, like rebuses, contain a combination of words, pictures, assorted letter-like limbs, and wing shells (pages 125, 131). They are constructed in imitation of those found in natural history museums. The death beetle appears many times in these boxes (pages 125, 127, 131), in one scene carrying the skull of an African bat (page 126). These fabrications echo the style but not the materials of traditional surrealist collage, in which souvenirs and scraps from the street have been assembled in a diary-like fashion. Even though I have a panoply of experiences surrounding the vastness of collections and of the finical classification systems practiced in museums, these boxes partake only in the most casual manner of personal memories. They represent a way of seeing similarities—and of writing with wire and beetle limbs.

In the studio, as a ruminator and fiddler I examine hoarded objects for signs of life, malleability, and metamorphic properties (pages 100, 101, 102, 104). But when these things are too small or unremarkable, or break apart, I do not attempt to restore them. Like clay or paint or words, they become the raw materials for invented scenarios; scraps become the stuff of fiction. Gnawed papers constitute the ingredients for this language of assemblage, and so, too, sand, stones, bones, pods, splinters of wood, and fragile metals.

My process of working with words and pictures is like assembling a masticated language; a rebus-language made of letters and images. I took a cue from the mouse (or mice) that had consumed half of *Flying Hostesses of the Air* (page 39) and assembled a structure of syllables and straw. I built new forms from fragments. When I was young, I used to tear and eat the corners of the books I read. Now, I don't personally chew any of the materials used in the assemblages. Termites have, the mice have, shipworms (teredos) too; it was natural for them to do so. My job is to rip, soak, break, align, realign, burnish, and glue.

The stones (page 51), cement blocks (pages 55, 56), soap (page 54), even the constructed insect boxes are like "things in books' clothing." Charles Lamb, who first used this phrase, was referring to those books he preferred not to see on the shelf: books by economists or boring tracts. Here, these things in books' clothing qualify—in the sense that they are in book disguise, the appearance of the book having been moved from one locus to another—as *translated*.

In the early 1980s, in response to an invitation by Polaroid Corporation to use its special large-format view cameras, I built a number of still-lifes designed to accommodate those cameras and their notoriously shallow depth of focus. A few times I got to use the biggest camera of all—a room at the Boston Museum of Fine Arts turned into a dark box. Inside the box we were three tiny beings looking in the direction of the lens and anticipated spectacle. When the shutter tripped and the lens opened, the scene flashed upside down across the retina and onto a six-foot-high negative. The shutter slammed shut, a guillotine, and the darkness resumed.

I selected World War One as a source for the "war windows" (page 121). The iconography of tanks and dirigibles and foot soldiers living in rat- and flea-laden mud trenches had a powerful effect on the imagination. Coincidentally I found a book of damaged vintage newspapers in an attic and so had reams of images to rip out from their sodden bindings and use, guilt free. I filled derelict windows with events composed from scraps of metal, glass, and miscellaneous printed materials, particularly the images from the front lines, and tinted scenes ripped from a tourist guidebook to the interior of the French château of Malmaison built by Napoleon for Josephine. The emperor's rooms are now visited by vagrant animals, often cattle or monkeys. Travelers and intruders pass through these scenes: soldiers

from the battlefields of the war (above), a spy peering through a hole in the desert-painted door onto Jerusalem (page 133), and a foot soldier grappling down (or up) a graffiti-laden wall (page 112). A reoccurring religious brother-hood, hooded and translucent, marches into burning cities, wanders over landscapes, and visits a museum re-created inside Malmaison (page 111). These men were forced to wander, and they had walked through many places, most of them during the Great War. Here, before a "painting" of the marching legs of a soldier the brotherhood pauses while one of them reads as if from a visitor's guidebook.

Every scene involves layers taken from separate historical strata and made to coexist. The cloisters, arches, and other vistas (page 116) come from images of Romanesque and Gothic churches and from a North African villa. Images of one bombed-out church layered upon another created a vista of arches beyond arches, which, when photographed, opened into apparent three-dimensional distances. While ripping and recombining scraps, I was practicing, as I do for such compositions, the lively art of interruption. Whatever occurs—a gaping archway, bombs falling—suggests not how it should be completed but what will happen next; I am *writing* the scenes in which monkeys and men in gas masks coexist (page 135) and in which animals corrupt imperial rooms (page 120). Recurring characters like the ghostly brotherhood establish fictional continuity. As they wander they spread the word and the news of that day.

In *The Great War and Modern Memory*, Paul Fussell writes, "Rumor . . . 'painted full of tongues' is in attendance as Shakespeare knew at every war." In the trenches there was widespread skepticism of official sources, so that "anything might be true except what was printed . . . It was as if the general human impulse to make fictions had been dramatically unleashed by the novelty, immensity and grotesqueness of the proceedings." Rumor, Fussell says, "was borne by . . . itinerant peddlers, jugglers, pilgrims, beggars."

For these theatrical scenes I used whatever it took to represent humanity: a mob, a corpse, a scarecrow: everyman reduced to an "it" in the landscape. "Stand over there," says a friend with a camera. "I need you to complete the vertical." As it happens, renunciation of one's first person singular becomes a wise adaptive strategy during any war. It is advisable at times of crisis to see oneself as a character on a stage. Fussell quotes from a scene in *Jim Hilton* by Stuart Cloete in which the protagonist, Hilton, wounded in the shoulder, makes his way back across the battlefield to retreat behind the lines:

> He was not here, he was somewhere else, on a high place looking down on
> a solitary figure picking its way between the shell holes. He thought, "that's
> young Captain Jim Hilton, that little figure. I wonder if he'll make it . . ."
> He was an observer, not a participant. It was always like that in war though

he had not realized it before. You were never you. . . . The "I" part of you was somewhere else.

In *Descent of Man* (page 119), the iconic march of the smallest monkey evolving through the apes and early man to us is shown in reverse order—like conscripts who have misread the compass. They are headed the wrong way, as if Homo sapiens came before the earlier forms and is now disappearing into the woods, consumed by the trees. As the history of war repeats itself, it becomes ever harder to distinguish between the wisdom of man and the instinct of beasts.

While composing these scenes I practiced the scales of image-text. This kind of "writing" involves projecting how a scene made of various two-dimensional layers will translate, when photographed, into the flat but apparent three-dimensional space of the picture. I can close one eye and see how the eroded levels meld to evoke apparent depth.

A collage (from *coller*, to glue) may be ready-made. Sometimes the gluing together is achieved by natural forces alone (page 43), a book soaked with vines, its Smythe-sewn spine fanning into a shape reminiscent of a tropical leaf first swollen and then compressed by rain or snow.

The image of the starving Buddha (page 115) comes from the guidebook to the museum in Lahore, Pakistan, where I first saw the statue. That the subject—transcendence into spirit—was made of bronze seemed paradoxical, since all that remains when one stops eating is, in fact, bones and spirit.

In the museum were three women wearing burkas, their eyes covered by woven window panels, reminiscent of jalousies, slatted blinds behind which, unseen, one can spy out upon the world. The women, along with the Buddha, were not meant to be of this world. They had come to see the statue, but how could they without also seeing threads of their embroidered peepholes?

Sometimes the easiest way to parse the memory of an event is to diagram it. I transferred an image of that Buddha onto a nineteenth-century print showing

the linear perspective of a cube in space, and that page, modestly chewed by termites, echoes the holes and hollows hunger leaves. It looks selectively burned and although one might equate this with immolation of the flesh, perhaps by fire, the explanation is less poetical—the scorched appearance of the paper is due to termite frass. The face of the Buddha fell within the inverted square but it has been worn away. Like a super-imposition of veil and spirit upon an event—far removed from what was there—this page is like a rubbing, a shadow draw-ing of the bronze.

While the page of the *Starving Buddha* (page 115) represents a reduction of a remem-bered scene, *Trouble at the Bottom of the Old Man's Garden* (above, and details, pages 46 and 47) is notable for its abun-dant accretion—of leaves, pods, and books. Here, galls, cracked or gaping, dis-gorge not seeds but texts—as if the pods were generating (artificial) progeny. From the scraps of words mighty libraries grow. *Trouble at the Bottom of the Old Man's Garden* was built in response to the way I felt one late summer day when wandering over eleven acres and mountains of discarded household objects, through lush tangles of vines and grasses. In this particular assemblage, I meant to convey the opulent excessiveness of a place overflowing with vegetable extravagance, which is why the work has a long title. The bearded man, fic-tional proprietor of the garden, appears in the far left-hand corner. There was so much; thicker layers lie below the layers you see and I forget now what was down there.

In Owls Head, Maine, I found a pile of cement slabs used to weigh down lobster traps when the latter were made of wooden slats. Newspapers that had caught the overflow of wet cement are now forever embedded in the matrix. Daily news, television schedules, and other advertising, thus set in stone, are still legible (pages 50, 55, 56, 64). "I can feel a tremendous pressure building up in my brain," reads one cartoon frame. It continues, "Then take the afternoon off, m'boy." The drawings of these characters have been effaced by saltwater and sand, obscured by barnacles and by whatever other vicissitudes may visit newspapers submerged in the north Atlantic year after year.

Accidental adherence—of a banknote to a fossil slab, stock market prices to cement, or the momentary touch-down of the cat's paws in a wet brick (page 59)—may forever alter a surface. I am the proud owner of this brick. It reminds me of a comic strip that, sadly, does not appear as an age-encrusted newspaper on any of the cement slabs but which, in reproduction elsewhere, rewards the soul. In George Herriman's *Krazy Kat* (1920s–30s) the story is always the same: the search and procurement of a brick by the mouse, Ignatz, the hurling of the brick by Ignatz at Krazy, which knocks him/her into a love-besotted stupor, the pursuit and incarceration of Ignatz by Officer Pupp. Here, Krazy is told by the Swami that many kinds of texts were found in bricks from "years agone"—"tomes in brick, news in brick, songs in brick, love letters in brick." The cat, for whom a blow from a brick hurled by Ignatz is a sign of true love, is fascinated by these revelations.

The story cycle, with its flow of ingenious, poetic language, landscapes that seem to be alive with cacti, trees, and anthropomorphic outcroppings, ever shifting as the story unfolds, is also a song—epic in length—about an obsessive *folie a*

deux. It is set in the land of Kaibito in the American Southwest, where natural formations, on the move like the prehistoric elephant-leg rocks that lumber from site to site, introduce titanic forces into the love-struck narrative of Krazy. The stars, the stones, even falling leaves (from the few deciduous trees remaining in this desert) provoke occasional monologues from one or another of the characters on the history of the earth and the movement of the stars. When a professor of anthropology unearths "a Paleocrystic love letter written by a maid a million years ago to a lad by the name of Job," brick is reconfirmed as an ancient substance that offers to Krazy proof of love and to the reader a sense of the primordial ooze from which inspiration and irrational affections rise. Then there's the knife that cannot help carving names in trees (pages 148, 149), the brush or pen that cannot resist revising a slogan painted on a wall (page 146), or the random stone that cannot help itself from being creased into the profile of a sleeping monkey (page 77).

Along with a brick bearing the imprints of cat paws (page 59), the lobster-pot slabs represent latter-day versions of ancient texts on stone from "years agone." The image on page 51 shows two stones remarkably similar to books. Along with volumes stiffened into clay-like slabs (page 73) or ones that curl up into a frail fan of pages at one end but turn into solidified sludge at the other (page 42), the stones belong to the collection of all these book-like objects.

The weather-beaten books in the studio include those more or less intact but dried shut into pulp bricks, almost impossible to open, certainly to read (pages 40, 41). The sight of these books comforts me. Owning them is restful because, as we were taught growing up, not to be "in a state of" reading, while reprehensible, could be forgiven if there was nothing there to read. A book that is still a book but cannot be read imparts peace and promise. The stones that look like books represent abstinence and convergence at their most satisfying.

Although ritualistic book burning to annihilate history represents one of mankind's more heinous activities, I find the creatively burned book (page 87), a black chrysanthemum, unexpectedly beautiful.

Two of the sixteenth-century scenes painted on the walls at the Château of Oiron demonstrate the depths inherent in the skin-like nature of the art of the fresco. In the first, Helen—the catalyst for the Trojan War—is pulled by her lover Paris in one direction and by her husband, Menelaus, in another. The paint has been so roughed up by the flaking texture of the plaster that the surface of the wall seems to be on the move, carrying the colors with it, and the struggle between the three principals appears to take place in a high wind. The second fresco, an enigmatic still-life, depicts a

large hare, native to France, inside a frame, staring at an Egyptian mongoose ("hycnefmon femelle") posed on a ledge below. The hare's gaze suggests some atavistic connection between the two animals. I hunt in books on natural history, French heraldry, biblical and medieval symbolism to find the significance of pairing the vicious (and, to the European, rare) mongoose with the wild hare. On and on the reading goes . . . Herein the trap of random research.

I tend to work from thrill to thrill. To know why the hare and mongoose appear together is not as compelling as the way they *look* painted: the hare's dark suspicious eyes, the splayed nails of the mongoose, the delicate thin colors, the mystery of perspective . . . for while seeming to occupy separate planes—one animal on a ledge and the other recessed—this is an illusion, as they are painted on one wall.

Photographers are aware of the chaos that plays outside the frame. In Agra, India, as I maneuvered the cubist blocks of color into position and at just the moment that the macaque hit the window frame, outside the field of view I kept at bay a swarm of street children pulling on my arm.

Sometimes I think that all the world's an altered page. When a scene in a town or countryside rises up as an artistically preassembled set, something tells me I was expecting this, that I knew it was there. About six hours from Anchorage—measured in dirt road miles—we reached the historic remains of a gold-processing plant. The staggered buildings on the ridge were collapsing into their interiors and into one another. Upright door and window frames were now oblique rectangles and squares, now ellipses creaking and twisting for a long time still.

I feel uneasy and also grateful that there are buildings caving in, books on the verge of illegibility, plants that flourish on volcanic slopes, collapses that trigger growth. Then—for a very short time—only three things count: the light, the camera, and things, holding . . .

Once, on a mountain pass in Bhutan, the minibus paused at a roadside Buddhist shrine. The outer walls were covered with ledges crowded with small clay crematoria, miniature stupas containing (perhaps even composed of) the ashes of the dead. Mesmerized by the writing on the walls, the colors of the paint and sculptural shapes, I circled the shrine, covering it from every angle with worshipful exposures. After a while, believing everyone to be back on board, the bus driver took off. I lay on the ground behind the shrine looking up at the ledges, anxiously protective of the film already exposed, despairing of the frames I would leave without. Rarely when traveling do I think, "This is it—this is the only time you will ever visit this place," but I did then. I was especially aware of the too-narrow field of view of a favorite lens and the hasty aggression of being a photographer. If the second minibus, forty minutes behind the first, had not arrived, I suppose I'd be there still.

Where is the glass that lies between recording and fabricating a landscape?
Wandering was achieved by placing two nineteenth-century glass plates of separate origin one on top of the other. This woman, nurse or nun, just passing through, is a phantom. When glass or plastic mediates the effect of natural light (pages 58, 89, 104, 107, 108, 141, 150–155), I feel the atmosphere of a deeper place. I think of the scene in Cocteau's film *Orpheo*, in which a young man strapped to a wooden frame, plying his trade, calls out *"verriere, verriere"* as he drifts through limbo. He is selling sheets of glass, penetrable by the dead, unpassable by the living. As a lover too of reflections, refractions, mirrors, and dissolution, I'd buy his wares any day.

1. Old Man's Garden

2. Pressure

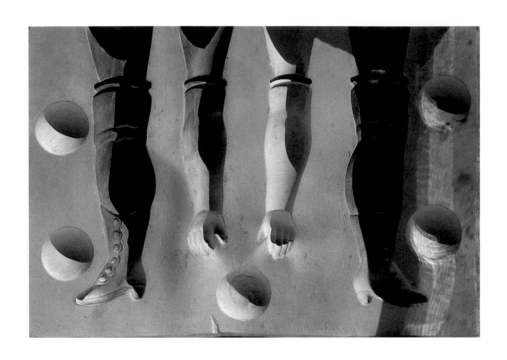

3. Dissolution

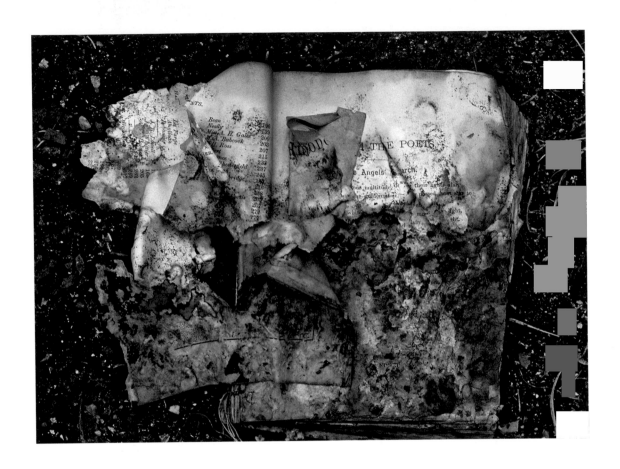

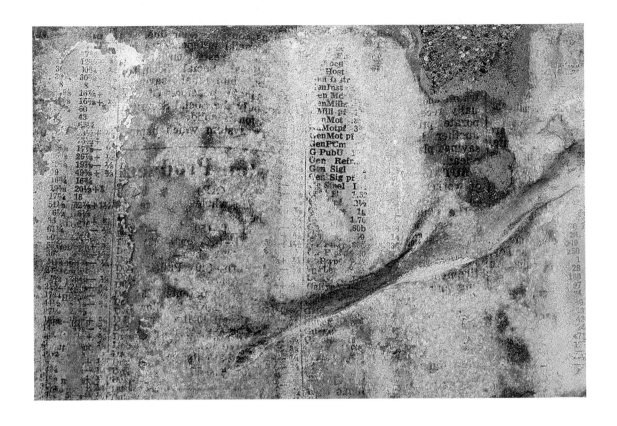

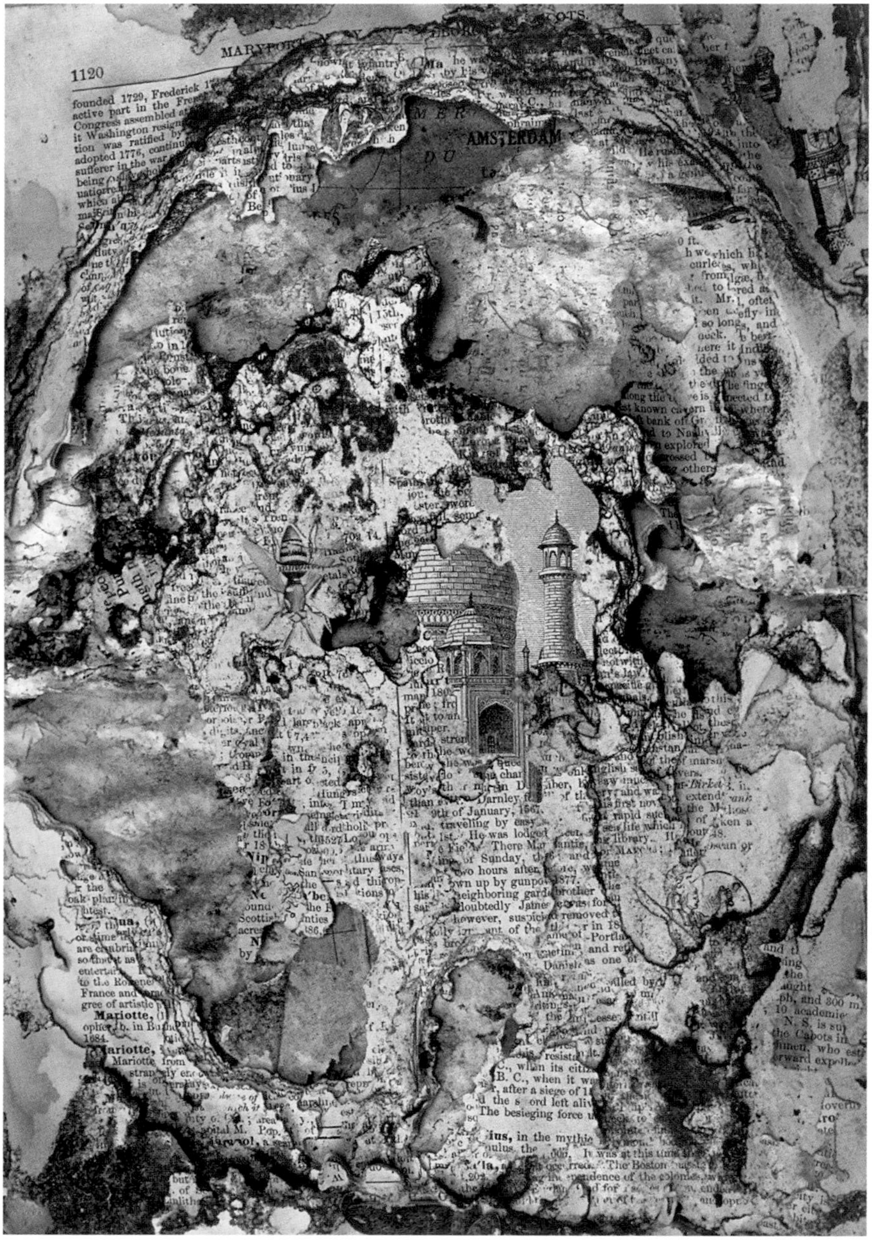
1120
AMSTERDAM
Mariotte,
The besieging force

69

4. Holes

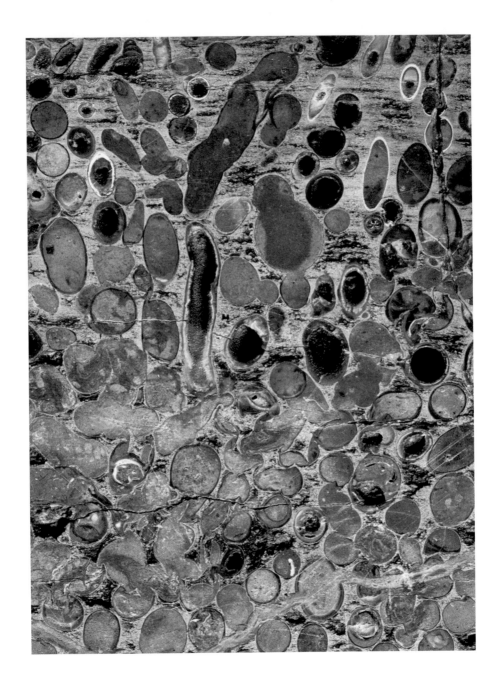

72

5. Scales

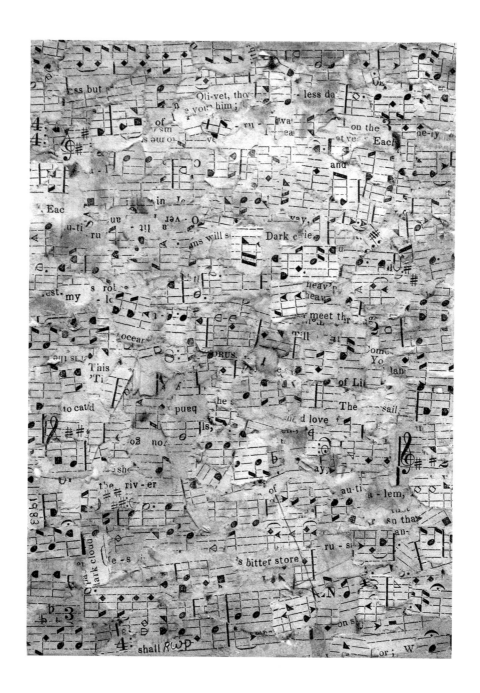

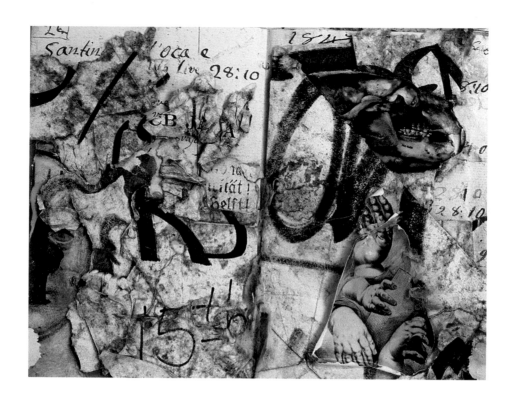

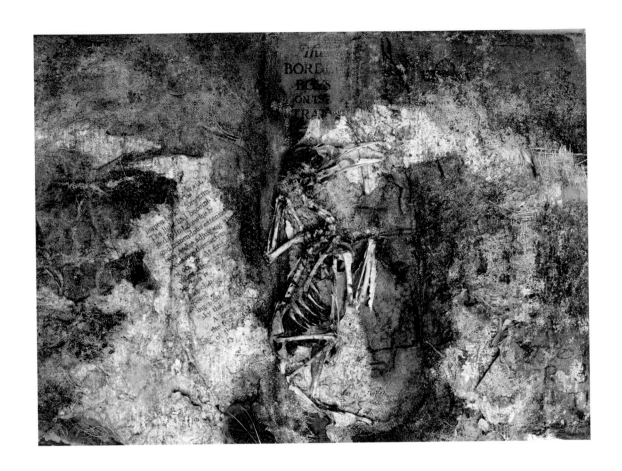

6. Skeleton

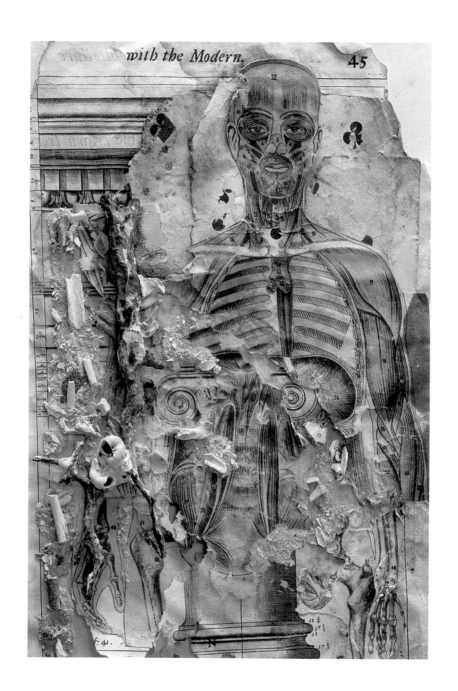

7. As Good As It Gets

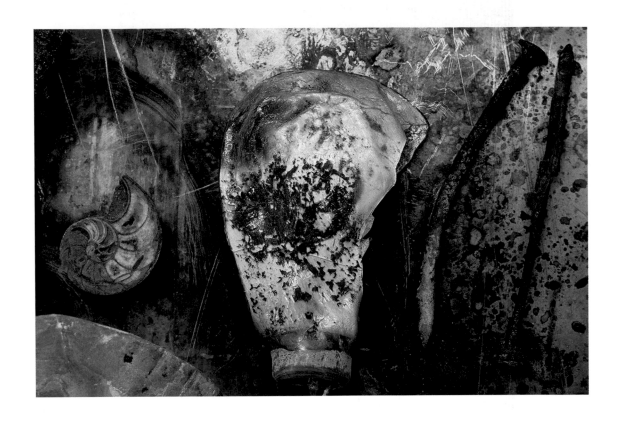

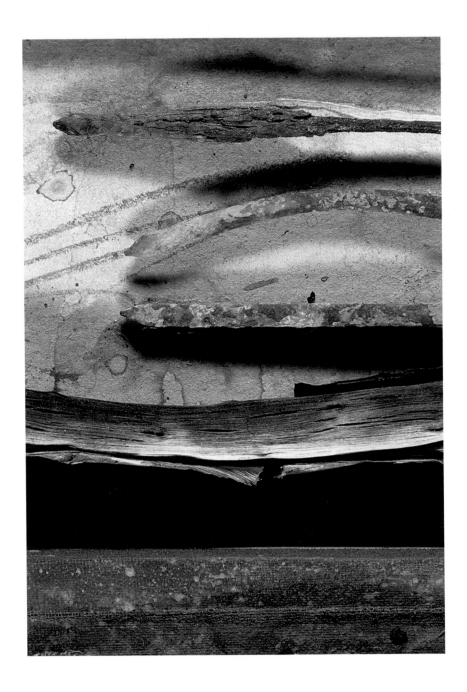

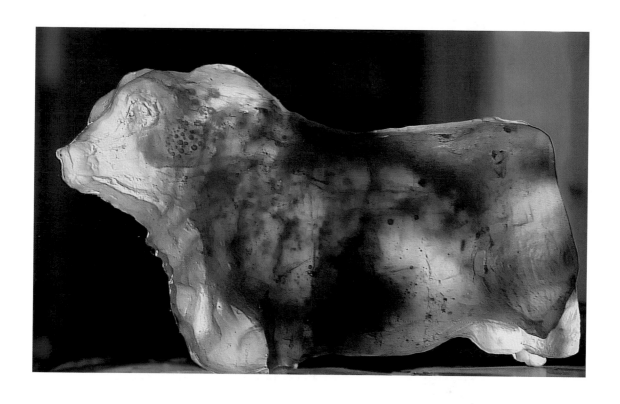

8. Hitting the Wall

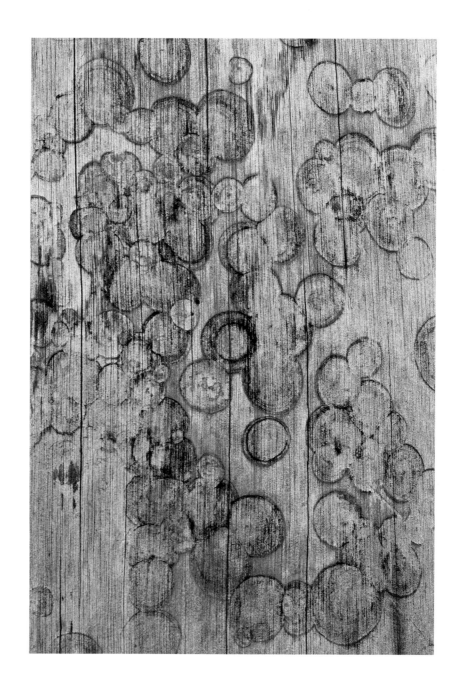

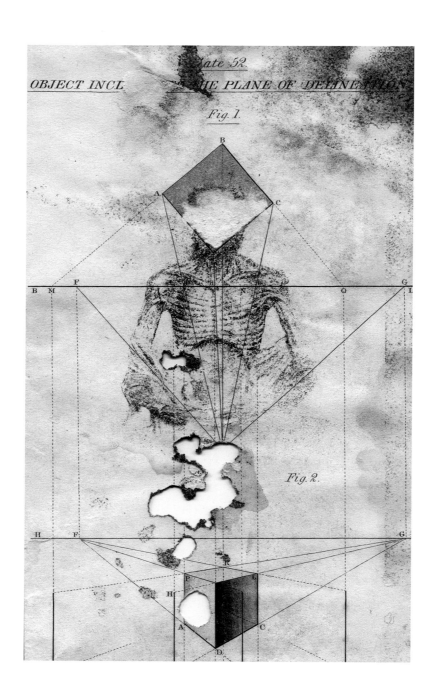

Plate 52.

OBJECT INCL   THE PLANE OF DELINEATION

Fig. 1.

Fig. 2.

115

9. Rebus

130

10. At the Same Time

11. Shalimar

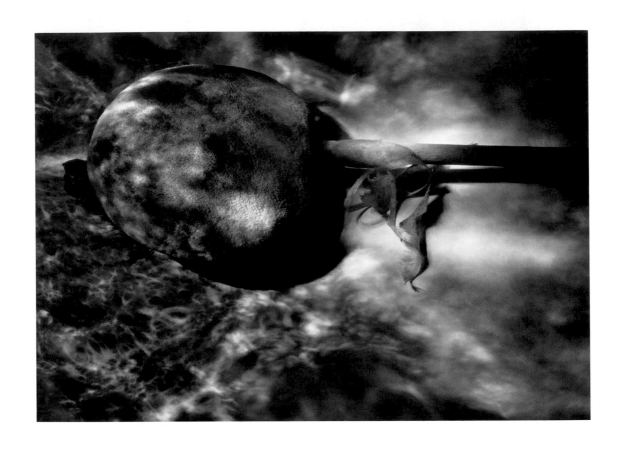

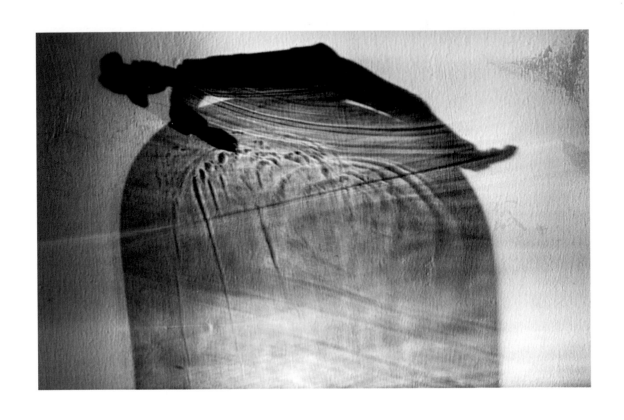

List of Illustrations

Sizes between 8 x 10 inches and 10 x 20 inches; 1–2 inches thick. Owls Head, Maine, 2003.

56 *"I feel a tremendous pressure building up in my brain,"* comic strip (Dagwood Bumstead) detail embedded in cement slab from lobster pot. Owls Head, Maine, 2003.

57 *Squashed rubber doll holding hand mirror,* approx. 5 inches high. Somerville, Mass., 2004.

58 *Arms and legs,* porcelain doll mold, approx. 18 x 10 inches. Somerville, Mass., 1998.

59 *Cat prints in brick.* Owls Head, Maine, 2005.

3. Dissolution

61 *By the author of "The Lower Part of the Sky,"* book cover, approx. 3½ x 8 inches. Owls Head, Maine, 1985.

62 *Among the Poets.* Owls Head, Maine, 1995.

63 Detail of *Among the Poets.* Owls Head, Maine, 1995.

64 *Stock Market,* cement block with newspaper stock market. Owls Head, Maine, 2005.

65 *Encyclopedia,* temporary assemblage, approx. 11 x 14 inches. Termite-eaten and water-damaged paper. Somerville, Mass., mid-1990s.

66 *Woman in the water,* snapshot (2 x 3 inches) found in vintage album. Owls Head, Maine, 1995.

67 *Book turned out of mud.* Owls Head, Maine, 2002.

68 *Play Goes Not Card Take,* photographed in situ. Owls Head, Maine, 2002.

69 *Book Run,* photographed in situ. Owls Head, Maine, 2002.

4. Holes

71 *Big Hole,* velvet picture frame over grass and torn tarpaulin. Owls Head, Maine, 2002.

72 *Teredo,* shipworm-damaged wood from original London Bridge, taken from the London Clay. Both wood and label (see page 24), at Sedgwick Museum, University of Cambridge, Cambridge, UK, 1992.

73 *Nails in book,* approx. 3 x 4 inches. Owls Head, Maine, 2000.

74 *Holes,* volcanic stones from Hawaiian beach, insect-damaged and poison-poxed box; 2 to 4 inches. Somerville, Mass., 2004.

75 *Bread from World War One,* approx. 3 inches square with broken edges. Bread and label authentic; bread shows insect damage and holes from preservatives. Presented to artist by the widow of the man to whom it was given. Medford, Mass., 2005.

76 *Buckle Tongues,* in two-hundred-year-old package, approx. 2 x 4 inches, 2 inches deep. Owls Head, Maine, 2003.

77 *Sleeping Monkey,* profile in stone, approx. 2–3 inches high. Owls Head, Maine, 2001.

5. Scales

79 *Bitter Store,* reworked music, collage, approx. 3 x 5 inches. Medford, Mass., early 1980s.

80 *Texas Rat,* with termite-eaten music. Somerville, Mass., 1990s.

81 *Leaves,* box of pages, approx. 3½ x 5 x ½ inches. Cambridge, Mass., 1989.

82 *Parrot emerging from language,* collage: foil, paper, wire, taxidermy, approx. 5½ x 8 inches, 1990s.

83 *Accretion* (object lost). Somerville, Mass., ca. 1998.

84 Detail from *"Letter to Mr. Spalding,"* collage of birch with letter fragments, mounted on board approx. 11 x 16 inches. Somerville, Mass., 1990s.

85 *Beetle Wings,* insect box collage of burned gauze, Italian and Chinese paper, scales and limbs of *Nicrophorus* beetle, 2¼ x 3 x ½ inches. Cambridge, Mass., 1989.

86 *The Border Boys on the Trail,* temporary assemblage: skeleton of bird on decrepit book. Somerville, Mass., ca. 2002.

87 *Dante's Inferno,* burned copy of Italian classic found on street outside University of Massachusetts, Boston, gift of the late artist Meryl Brater in 1989. Photograph, Somerville, Mass., ca. 1995.

6. Skeleton

89 *Foucault's Pendulum,* paperback book eaten by termites in Bali, approx. 4 x 5½ inches. Somerville, Mass., 1996.

90 *Book for Fishes,* artifact owned by Museum of Comparative Zoology, Harvard University. Somerville, Mass., mid-1990s.

91 *Owl,* bird skeleton found in fireplace, gift of J. Seeley, mid-1980s. Middletown, Connecticut, 2005.

92 *"Letter to Mr. Spalding,"* termite-eaten letter (approx. 2 x 3½ inches) on advertising tin. Somerville, Mass., 1990s.

93 *With the Modern,* collage, approx. 8 x 10 inches; architectural anatomical texts, playing cards, bones from Madagascar. Somerville, Mass., early 1990s.

94 *Religions of the World,* detail, collage; fragments of books, termite paper, Haitian cross, seal gut. Somerville, Mass., mid-1990s.

95 *Cicadas,* on damaged book to which foreign-language texts have been added. Temporary assemblage, 1990s.

96 *Wood.* Woods Hole, Mass., 2006.

97 *Moths and music,* collage, 2¼ x 3½ inches; termite-eaten music and white moths. Cambridge, Mass., 1989.

7. As Good As It Gets

99 *Bird in Motion.* Somerville, Mass., 2005.

100 *Typewriter.* Owls Head, Maine, 1990s.

101 *Obie's Phone,* phone rescued from shop fire. Somerville, Mass., 2005.

102 *Lightbulb from Malibu,* with nails from visitors' center in Hawaii, ammonite, oxidized metal. Temporary assemblage. Somerville, Mass., ca. 2002.

103 *Croquet Balls,* in battery case "GOULD." Somerville, Mass., 2005.

104 *Shadows,* bird from chimney fire, fish, mysterious blades. Somerville, Mass., 1990s.

105 *Bird-headed figure,* burned aluminum foil. Somerville, Mass., 2006.

106 *Disaster Kit*, nails from Hawaii lava flow, wood from Malibu fires. Temporary assemblage. Somerville, Mass., mid-1990s.

107 *Balance*, neolithic rock. Medford, Mass., 2006.

108 *Irish Mail*. Medford, Mass., 2006.

109 *Glass bull*, cast by the artist Mark Lorenzi from an old toy pulled out of mud. Photograph Medford, Mass., 2006.

8. Hitting the Wall

111 *Brotherhood Visits the Museum*, one-quarter detail from original collage *Page 2*, approx. 3½ x 5 x 2½–3 inches; book cloth, wire, translucent transfer print, and vintage newspaper, behind leaded glass pane. Photographed as 20 x 24–inch Polaroid Land print. Cambridge, Mass., 1985.

112 *Soldier climbing down or up the wall*, detail (upper left quadrant), from *Malmaison #1*, approx. 3 x 5 inches; collage: cut paper illustrations, vintage World War One newspapers. Photographed as 20 x 24–inch Polaroid Land print, 1985.

113 *Circles*. Woods Hole, Mass., 2006.

114 *Gas box*. Florence, Italy, 1993.

115 *Geometry and Starving Buddha*, from museum in Islamabad, Pakistan, approx. 6 x 8 inches; ink transfer on nineteenth-century page, termite damage. Somerville, Mass., 1989.

116 *Ape in Archway*, detail from *Malmaison #1* (upper left quadrant), approx. 3 x 5 inches; collage: cut paper illustrations, vintage World War One newspapers. Photographed as 20 x 24–inch Polaroid Land print, 1985.

117 *Sleeping orangutan*, bones from Madagascar, construction, 7 x 12 inches. Somerville, Mass., photograph ca. 1992.

118 *Oscar off Pedestal*, chocolate in foil, tin. Medford, Mass., 2006.

119 *Descent of Man enters the woods*, middle frame detail from original collage *Traveling*; metal, mica, glass, torn paper scene. Translucent transfer print photographed as 20 x 24–inch Polaroid Land print. Cambridge, Mass., 1985.

120 *Knight in chapel*, one-sixth detail from original collage *Eve*, approx. 5 x 7 inches; photograph, paper, vintage newspaper in wooden window frame. Photographed as 20 x 24–inch Polaroid Land print. Cambridge, Mass., 1985.

121 *Airship*, detail (lower right sixth) from original collage *Eve*, approx. 8 x 10 inches; torn paper scene, wire, mica layers, vintage World War One newspaper prints in wooden window frame. Photographed as 20 x 24–inch Polaroid Land print. Cambridge, Mass., 1985.

9. Rebus

123 *Cocoons*, collage, 5 x 7 inches; fossil bivalves, termite-eaten paper, mammal tooth, insect fragments. Cambridge, Mass. 1989.

124 *Writing Exercise, "1847,"* collage, 2¼ x 3 x ½ inches; Italian account book, Chinese text, limbs and carapaces of burying beetles, cicada, mouse skull. Somerville, Mass., 1989–90.

125 *Causality*, collage, approx. 2 x 4 x ¼ inches; book parts, various added texts, and thin wings of butterfly. Somerville, Mass., 1990s.

126 *Seed Catalogue*, detail of 48-panel construction measures approx. 3 x 5 feet. Materials include metal, bone, beetle, rice paper, cardboard gaming discs, discarded museum label, and deaccessioned fossil. Somerville, Mass., 1990.

127 *Rye*, insect box, 2¼ x 3 x ½ inches; insects, various papers. Somerville, Mass., 1989.

128–129 *War Games*, left- and right-hand panels from collage of mica, paper wasp nest, leaves, glass watch parts, multiple reproductions of museum specimen of hanging ape, World War One newspaper pictures; 20 x 24–inch photograph. Medford, Mass., 1985.

130 *Rebus*, insect box with beetle limb marks, 2¼ x 3 x ½ inches; decorative paper, Chinese text, limbs of *Nicrophorus* beetle. Cambridge, Mass., 1989.

131 *At*, insect box, 2¼ x 3 x ½ inches; butterfly wing parts, yellow thorax, Chinese text, and cotton. Cambridge, Mass., 1989.

10. At the Same Time

133 *Spying on Jerusalem*, detail, approx. 2 x 3 inches; collage: reverse glass painting, tinfoil, World War One newspaper. Object no longer exists intact. Somerville, Mass., mid-1990s.

134 *Ganai Coach*, painted scene on truck. Pakistan, 1989.

135 Detail of *Enola Gay*, approx. 7 x 12–inch collage on reverse glass painting, monkeys, men in gas masks. Medford, Mass., 1984.

136 *Luck of the Draw*, collage of World War One newsprint and playing card, approx. 11 x 14 inches. Original legend reads: "Bombing Montmedy, 42 kilometers north of Verdun, while the First Army advances in the Meuse-Argonne Sector. Three bombs, loaded with T.N.T., have been released by an aviator belonging to the 11th Air Squadron. One bomb has already hit the railhead and two are speeding on their errand of destruction. That the Germans are making desperate efforts to wing the plane is shown by the two black puffs of smoke indicating the explosion of anti-aircraft shells. To the right may be seen a Red Cross on the roof of a building. The aviator respected it. This remarkable photograph was taken by a member of the 96th Air Squadron." Somerville, Mass., 1990s.

137 *Landscape of Scrap Metal*, detail of studio wall, approx. 3 x 2 feet. Somerville, Mass., 2005.

138 *In the Hollow*, 150-year-old pressed orchid placed in termite-eaten hollow paperback book. Somerville, Mass., 2000.

139 *French village with trouble rising*, collage of World War One newsprint and rusted metal, approx. 11 x 14 inches. Somerville, Mass., 1990s. Original legend reads: "After peace had come to Saint Mihiel. The town was not badly damaged as it was never under direct artillery fire, although air bombs destroyed that part of the town lying close to the river. Chauvoncourt, just

across the Meuse, was completely destroyed. Early in the war the French made an attempt to drive the Germans out of the village, but the attacking force was annihilated by a subterranean mine." (Photo U.S. Air Service, ca. 1918.)

140 *Mount Rushmore with lips*, one-sixth detail from *Write a Letter to Your Congressman*, approx. 8 x 10 inches; metal, photography, glass, found artwork, and wood. Polaroid Land print, 20 x 24 inches. Cambridge, Mass., 1989.

141 *Grail*, photograph of termite-eaten paperback, *Foucault's Pendulum,* with petrified egg yolk, refracted light. Somerville, Mass., 1996.

142 *Institution for Women, New Hampshire*, approx. 2 x 3½ inches, detail of collage commemorating prison, with found illustrations, portrait of monkey specimen, wire, metal, glue. Photographed as 20 x 24–inch Polaroid Land print. Cambridge, Mass., 1984.

143 *Benediction*, soap, glass, footlight. Medford, Mass., 2005.

11. Shalimar

145 *Sati*, handprints on wall. Agra, India, 1989.

146 *Karakoram*, superimposed graffiti (Chinese then Urdu) with rock, by highway. Pakistan, 1989.

147 Roadside shrine with clay cremation "stupas." Bhutan, 1989.

148 *"Anoop."* Shalimar Gardens, Srinagar, India, 1989. (Like "Anjil" of *Krazy Kat.*)

149 *Accidental Bird*. Shalimar Gardens, Srinagar, India, 1989.

150 *Christina's Powder Puff*, belonged to subject of Andrew Wyeth's *Christina's World*, found wedged in Maine window, 2005.

151 *Mandrake*, root from Bhutan, 1989, approx. 10 inches tall. Medford, Mass., 2006.

152 *Sleep*. Medford, Mass., 2006. Published in *Conjunctions* 46, spring 2006.

153 *Wait*, Oscar with pedestal, chocolate in foil, tin. Medford, Mass., 2006.

154 *Ephemera*, insect display, museum, Khana, India, 1984. Published in *Conjunctions* 46, spring 2006.

155 *Delivery*. Medford, Mass., 2006. Published in *Conjunctions* 46, spring 2006.

156 *Fish on Music*, cleared and stained fish in glycerin on medieval music, American Museum of Natural History, New York City, 1990.